Inspiring Quotes From Inspiring Women

Katie Johnson

© Copyright 2019 - All rights reserved.

The content contained within this book may not be reproduced, duplicated or transmitted without direct written permission from the author or the publisher. Under no circumstances will any blame or legal responsibility be held against the publisher, or author, for any damages, reparation, or monetary loss due to the information contained within this book. Either directly or indirectly. You are responsible for your own choices, actions, and results.

Legal Notice:

This book is copyright protected. This book is only for personal use. You cannot amend, distribute, sell, use, quote or paraphrase any part, or the content within this book, without the consent of the author or publisher.

Disclaimer Notice:

Please note the information contained within this document is for educational and entertainment purposes only. All effort has been executed to present accurate, up to date, and reliable, complete information. No warranties of any kind are declared or implied. Readers acknowledge that the author is not engaging in the rendering of legal, financial, medical or professional advice. The content within this book has been derived from various sources. Please consult a licensed professional before attempting any techniques outlined in this book.

By reading this document, the reader agrees that under no circumstances is the author responsible for any losses, direct or indirect, which are incurred as a result of the use of the information contained within this document, including, but not limited to, — errors, omissions, or inaccuracies.

Table Of Contents

Mother Teresa 1
Anne Frank 2
Elinor Ostrom 3
Rosalind Franklin 4
Grace Hopper 5
Sarah Breedlove 6
Catherine de Medici 7
Bessie Coleman 8
Boudicca 9
Diana 10
Coco Chanel 11
Virginia Woolf 12
Anna Jacobson Schwartz 13
George Eliot 14
Mary Somerville 15
Sarojini Naidu 16
Dowager Empress Cixi 17
Isabella of Castile 18
Fanny Mendelssohn 19
Katia Krafft 20
Mary Shelley 21
Annette Kellerman 22
Jane Austen 23
Ada Lovelace 24
Eleanor of Aquitaine 25

Rosa Parks 26
Susan Sontag 27
Hypatia 28
Artemisia Gentileschi 29
Cleopatra 30
Emmeline Pankhurst 31
Maria Merian 32
Josephine Butler 33
Indira Gandhi 34
Estée Lauder 35
Wangari Maathai 36
Mary Seacole 37
Anna Akhmatova 38
Mary Wollstonecraft 39
Mary Anning 40
Marie Curie 41
Joan of Arc 42
Sirimavo Bandaranaike 43
Clara Schumann 44
Sonja Henie 45
Gwen John 46
Elizabeth Fry 47
Joan Robinson 48
Emily Hobhouse 49
Lise Meitner 50

Table Of Contents

Marie Stopes 51
Simone de Beauvoir 52
Maryam Mirzakhani 53
Emilie du Chatelet 54
Nellie Bly 55
Frida Kahlo 56
Wilma Rudolph 57
Aphra Behn 58
Catherine of Siena 59
Suzanne Lenglen 60
Queen Victoria 61
Fanny Burney 62
Isabella Bird 63
Junko Tabei 64
Theodora 65
Fanny Blankers-Koen 66
Margaret Thatcher 67
Zora Neale Hurston 68
Gabriela Mistral 69
Catherine the Great 70
Sacagawea 71
Katharine Graham 72
Ethel Smyth 73
Marie Marvingt 74
Yeshe Tsogyal 75

Florence Nightingale 76
Andrea Dworkin 77
Beulah Louise Henry 78
Eleanor Rathbone 79
Murasaki Shikibu 80
Eleanor Roosevelt 81
Sojourner Truth 82
Eva Perón 83
Golda Meir 84
Corazon Aquino 85
Millicent Fawcett 86
Rosa Luxemburg 87
Benazir Bhutto 88
Marie Antoinette 89
Hildegard of Bingen 90
Ida Bell Wells-Barnett 91
Emily Murphy 92
Harriet Tubman 93
Kate Sheppard 94
Olympe de Gouges 95
Christina 96
Madame de Stael 97
Sophie Germain 98
Jane Addams 99
Saint Teresa of Ávila 100

Mother Teresa

(26 August 1910 - 5 September 1997)

Mother Teresa was the founder of the Order of the Missionaries of Charity, a Roman Catholic congregation of women dedicated to helping the poor. Considered one of the 20th Century's greatest humanitarians, she was canonized as Saint Teresa of Calcutta in 2016.

"If you want to change the world, go home and love your family."

"Peace begins with a smile on your face."

"Spread love everywhere you go. Let no one ever come to you without leaving happier."

Anne Frank

(12 June 1929 - February 1945)

Annelies Marie Frank was a German-born Dutch-Jewish diarist. One of the most discussed Jewish victims of the Holocaust, she gained fame posthumously with the publication of The Diary of a Young Girl, in which she documents her life in hiding from 1942 to 1944, during the German occupation of the Netherlands in World War II. It is one of the world's best known books and has been the basis for several plays and films.

"I still believe, in spite of everything, that people are truly good at heart."

"What a wonderful thought it is that some of the best days of our lives haven't even happened yet."

"Parents can only give good advice or put them on the right paths, but the final forming of a person's character lies in their own hands."

Elinor Ostrom

(7 August 1933 - 12 June 2012)

Elinor Claire "Lin" Ostrom was an American political economist. She was the only woman to have won the top prize in Economics. Ostrom trained as a political scientist after she was rejected for an Economics PhD because she lacked maths training. She was awarded the Nobel Prize in 2009, shared with Oliver Williamson, for her work that showed how commonly owned property such as forests can be used cooperatively and not over-used as economists assumed.

"The power of a theory is exactly proportional to the diversity of situations it can explain."

"Therein is the tragedy. Each man is locked into a system that compels him to increase his herd without limit – in a world that is limited. Ruin is the destination toward which all men rush, each pursuing his own best interest in a society that believes in the freedom of the commons."

Rosalind Franklin

(25 July 1920 - 16 April 1958)

Rosalind Franklin was a British scientist. When the double helix structure of DNA was discovered, scientists claimed that they had unravelled the secret of life itself. The crucial piece of evidence was provided by the expert crystallographer Rosalind Franklin – the famous photograph 51, an X-ray picture showing a dark cross of dots, the signature image of a concealed molecular spiral.

"In my view, all that is necessary for faith is the belief that by doing our best we shall succeed in our aims: the improvement of mankind."

"Science and everyday life cannot and should not be separated."

"Science, for me, gives a partial explanation for life. In so far as it goes, it is based on fact, experience and experiment."

Grace Hopper

(9 December 1906 - 1 January 1992)

Grace Hopper was a Computer Scientist. When electronic computers began to revolutionise society, Grace Hopper was one of the leading players, having already become the first woman to earn a PhD in mathematics from Yale University in 1934. First at Harvard, and then in the US Navy, Hopper worked on the very earliest computers and later developed COBOL, the commercial programming language that enabled a military innovation to transform the business world.

"If it's a good idea, go ahead and do it. It's much easier to apologize than it is to get permission."

"We're flooding people with information. We need to feed it through a processor. A human must turn information into intelligence or knowledge. We've tended to forget that no computer will ever ask a new question."

"You don't manage people, you manage things. You lead people."

Sarah Breedlove

(23 December 1867 - 25 May 1919)

Sarah Breedlove was an entrepreneur and activist. She was the first self-made female millionaire in America. She developed a line of beauty and hair products for African-Americans. Her Madam C.J. Walker Manufacturing Company made her one of the most successful African-American business owners in history.

"Don't sit down and wait for the opportunities to come. Get up and make them."

"I got myself a start by giving myself a start."

"I have made it possible for many colored women to abandon the wash-tub for more pleasant and profitable occupations."

Catherine de Medici

(13 April 1519 - 5 January 1589)

Catherine de Medici was an Italian-born Queen of France and mother of three kings. She held a hugely influential position in the nation's politics throughout the 16th century. Civil war and religious tensions often led her to take drastic measures, yet she is also remembered for her tenacious nature and artistic patronage.

"History is written by survivors, and I am surely that."

"The first lesson I ever learned was never to wait for a man's rescue."

"A false report, if believed during three days, may be of great service to a government."

Bessie Coleman

(26 January 1892 - 10 April 1926)

Bessie Coleman was a civil aviator. In 1921, Coleman became the first American woman to earn an international pilot's license, despite racial discrimination preventing her entry to American flying schools. After travelling to France to earn her licence, Coleman returned to America where racial and gender bias prevented her from becoming a commercial pilot. Stunt flying was her only option and she staged the first public flight by an African-American woman in the US, on 3 September 1922. Coleman drew huge crowds to her shows, refusing to perform before segregated audiences and raising money to found a school to train black aviators.

"The air is the only place free from prejudices."

"I don't know who invented high heels, but all women owe him a lot."

"I decided blacks should not have to experience the difficulties I had faced, so I decided to open a flying school and teach other black women to fly".

Boudicca

(c30 - 61)

Boudicca was the Queen of the Iceni tribe during the Roman occupation of Britain. In either 60 or 61 AD, Boudicca united different tribes in a Celtic revolt against Roman rule. Leading an army of around 100,000, she succeeded in driving the Romans out of modern-day Colchester (then capital of Roman Britain), London and Verulamium (St Albans). Her success led Roman emperor Nero to consider withdrawing from Britain entirely, until the Roman governor, Paullinus, finally defeated her in a battle in the West Midlands.

"I am not fighting for my kingdom and wealth now. I am fighting as an ordinary person for my lost freedom, my bruised body, and my outraged daughters."

"If you weigh well the strengths of our armies you will see that in this battle we must conquer or die. This is a woman's resolve. As for the men, they may live or be slaves."

Diana

(1 July 1961 - 31 August 1997)

In 1981, Diana Spencer became the first wife of the heir apparent to the British throne, Charles, Prince of Wales. She became well known internationally for her charity work for sick children, the banning of landmines, and for raising awareness about those affected by cancer, HIV/AIDS and mental illness.

"I don't go by the rule book... I lead from the heart, not the head."

"I like to be a free spirit. Some don't like that, but that's the way I am."

"Carry out a random act of kindness, with no expectation of reward, safe in the knowledge that one day someone might do the same for you."

Coco Chanel

(19 August 1883 - 10 January 1971)

Coco Chanel was a French Fashion Designer. She emerged from a difficult, nomadic childhood in France to become an internationally famous designer, whose eponymous brand spans fashion, jewellery and perfume. Her importance and contributions to female fashion is complicated by her suspected collaboration with German intelligence operations during the Second World War.

"In order to be irreplaceable one must always be different."

"A girl should be two things: classy and fabulous."

"Don't spend time beating on a wall, hoping to transform it into a door."

Virginia Woolf

(25 January 1882 - 28 March 1941)

Virginia Woolf was a British Modern Novelist, most famous for her works including Mrs Dalloway and A Room of One's Own. She was also one of the founders of the influential literary set the Bloomsbury Group. Her complex personal life and sometimes controversial viewpoints have led her to become both an influential and divisive figure.

"For most of history, Anonymous was a woman."

"If you do not tell the truth about yourself you cannot tell it about other people."

"Women have served all these centuries as looking-glasses possessing the magic and delicious power of reflecting the figure of man at twice its natural size."

Anna Schwartz

(11 November 1915 - 21 June 2012)

Anna Jacobson Schwartz was an American economist. She was the co-author of the seminal book that changed our understanding of the Great Depression and how to prevent it from happening again. A Monetary History of the United States: 1867-1960, written with Nobel Prize laureate Milton Friedman, showed that it was monetary policy that caused the Great Crash of 1929 and the subsequent drastic depression.

"The contraction from 1929 to 1933 was by far the most severe business-cycle contraction during the near-century of U.S. history we cover and it may well have been the most severe in the whole of U.S. history."

"Why is easy monetary policy such a sin? Because in such an environment, loans are cheap and borrowers can finance every project that they dream up. This results in excesses, and also increases the severity of the recession that inevitably follows when the bubble bursts."

George Eliot

(22 November 1819 - 22 December 1880)

George Eliot was a Novelist and Poet. The 19th-century novelist and poet Mary Anne Evans, born in Warwickshire, took the pen name George Eliot in a bid to have her work taken seriously. Her subsequent novels, including Middlemarch and Slias Marner, tackle weighty themes including religion, marriage and industrialisation.

"Life began with waking up and loving my mother's face."

"Animals are such agreeable friends - they ask no questions, they pass no criticisms."

"It will never rain roses: when we want to have more roses, we must plant more roses."

Mary Somerville

(26 December 1780 - 29 November 1872)

Mary Somerville was a science writer and polymath. In Victorian Britain, Mary was celebrated as 'The Queen of the Sciences.' Her research was published in the Royal Society's prestigious journal, her interpretation of complex French astronomy became a standard textbook, and her syntheses of scientific knowledge communicated the latest discoveries to public audiences. Although unable to go to university herself, the Oxford college named after her opened the doors to women's education. In 2017, Somerville's contribution to science was recognised by the Royal Bank of Scotland, which featured her on its new plastic £10 note.

"The most savage people are also the ugliest."

"The moral disposition of the age appears in the refinement of conversation."

"No circumstance in the natural world is more inexplicable than the diversity of form and color in the human race."

Sarojini Naidu

(13 February 1879 - 2 March 1949)

Sarojini Naidu was a political activist and poet. As a freedom fighter and poet, she was the first Indian woman to be president of the Indian National Congress and to be appointed an Indian state governor. A close friend of Mohandas Gandhi, in 1917 Naidu helped found the Women's India Association and later played a leading role in the civil disobedience movement in colonial India. Two years before her death, India gained its independence as a sovereign nation, becoming the largest democracy in the world.

"A country's greatness lies in its undying ideals of love and sacrifice that inspire the mothers of the race."

"When there is oppression, the only self-respecting thing is to rise and say this shall cease today, because my right is justice. If you are stronger, you have to help the weaker boy or girl both in play and in the work."

Dowager Empress Cixi

(29 November 1835 - 15 November 1908)

Dowager Empress was a Chinese ruler for 47 years. One of the most powerful women in Chinese history, Empress Cixi rose from low-ranking concubine of the Xianfeng emperor to regent of China for nearly 50 years. During her regency, Cixi oversaw a number of economic and military reforms which helped transform China into a more modern world power, although the political murders carried out during her reign and her role in the Boxer Rebellion have cast a shadow over her reputation.

"Your tail, is becoming too heavy to wag."

"Whoever makes me unhappy for a day, I will make suffer a lifetime."

"Now they [the Powers] have started the aggression, and the extinction of our nation is imminent. If we just fold our arms and yield to them, I would have no face to see our ancestors after death. If we must perish, why not fight to the death?"

Isabella of Castile

(22 April 1451 - 26 November 1504)

Isabella was the Queen of Castile, a political unifier, and an economic reformer. Isabella I was a hugely important figure in 15th-century Spain. Together with her husband, she was responsible for less savoury episodes, including the forced expulsion of Muslim and Jewish subjects, yet she remains a key figure in the nation's rise to become an early global superpower.

"The distance is great from the firm belief to the realization from concrete experience."

"I will assume the undertaking for my own crown of Castile, and am ready to pawn my jewels to defray the expenses of it, if the funds in the treasury should be found inadequate."

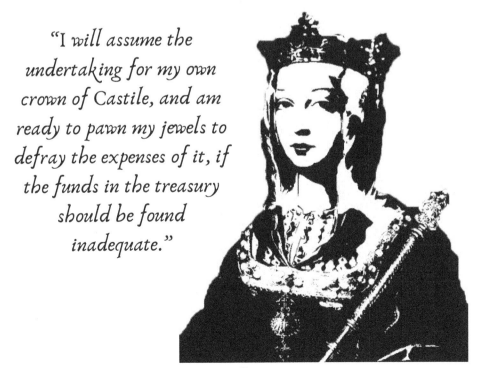

Fanny Mendelssohn

(14 November 1805 - 14 May 1847)

Fanny Mendelssohn was a German pianist and composer, whose hundreds of works include songs, sonatas and a piano trio. The oldest of four children, including fellow composer Felix, her output is praised by critics for its energy and melodicism.

"It must be a sign of talent that I do not give up, though I can get nobody to take an interest in my efforts."

"If nobody ever offers an opinion or takes the slightest interest in one's production, one loses not only all pleasure in them, but all power of judging their value."

"Thus far, but no farther."

Katia Krafft

(17 April 1942 - 3 June 1991)

Katia Krafft was a French volcanologist. She travelled the world to the edges of human survival, devoting her life to documenting volcanoes and volcanic eruptions in photos and film. Her work was instrumental in gaining the cooperation of local authorities and encouraging them to evacuate the areas surrounding active volcanos. Krafft and her volcanologist husband were both killed while filming the eruption of Mount Unzen in Japan, in 1991.

"I have seen so many eruptions in the last 20 years that I don't care if I die tomorrow."

"It's very nice to feel. You're nothing. You're just nothing when you're near a volcano."

"I would always like to be near craters, drunk with fire, gas, my face burned by the heat.... It's not that I flirt with my death, but at this point I don't care about it, because there is the pleasure of approaching the beast and not knowing if he is going to catch you."

Mary Shelley

(30 August 1797 - 1 February 1851)

Mary Shelley was a novelist. Born to political philosopher William Godwin and feminist activist Mary Wollstonecraft, and husband of poet Percy Bysshe Shelley, Mary Shelley managed to make a name for herself, even in such high-achieving company. Blending the horrific with the sympathetic, the Gothic with the Romantic, the novel has gone on to become a literary classic.

"I do not wish women to have power over men; but over themselves."

"The beginning is always today."

"Nothing contributes so much to tranquilize the mind as a steady purpose - a point on which the soul may fix its intellectual eye."

Annette Kellerman

(6 July 1887 - 5 November 1975)

Annette Kellerman was an Australian professional swimmer. She combined competitive racing and distance feats with aquatic exhibitions, the forerunner of modern synchronised swimming. Kellerman successfully campaigned for rational dress in the sport, facing arrest for indecency in the US for wearing a revolutionary one-piece swimsuit. As well as popularising the modern swimming costume, Kellerman also appeared in films and wrote books and articles on swimming and health.

"Swimming cultivates imagination; the man with the most is he who can swim in his solitary course day or night and forget a black earth full of people that push".

"The man who has not given himself completely to the sun and winds and cold sting of the waves will never know all the meanings of life."

Jane Austen

(16 December 1775 - 18 July 1817)

Jane Austen was one of the most famous figures in British history thanks to her novels. Often lacing plots exploring marriage, status and social sensibility with a distinctive irony, her works have been adapted many times in plays, films and TV series.

"Friendship is certainly the finest balm for the pangs of disappointed love."

"There is no charm equal to tenderness of heart."

"A lady's imagination is very rapid; it jumps from admiration to love, from love to matrimony in a moment."

Ada Lovelace

(10 December 1815 - 27 November 1852)

Augusta Ada King, Countess of Lovelace was an English mathematician and writer, chiefly known for her work on Charles Babbage's proposed mechanical general-purpose computer, the Analytical Engine.

"The more I study, the more insatiable do I feel my genius for it to be."

"Understand well as I may, my comprehension can only be an infinitesimal fraction of all I want to understand."

"The intellectual, the moral, the religious seem to me all naturally bound up and interlinked together in one great and harmonious whole."

Eleanor of Aquitaine

(1122 - 1 April 1204)

Eleanor of Aquitaine was one of the wealthiest women of the Middle Ages – and one of its most eligible brides. Eleanor of Aquitaine married Louis VII of France and then, following their divorce, the future Henry II of England. As such, she occupies a singularly important position in the medieval histories of both countries.

"Trees are not known by their leaves, nor even by their blossoms, but by their fruits".

"Grief is not very different from illness: in the impetus of its fire it does not recognise lords, it does not fear colleagues, it does not respect or spare anyone, not even itself".

"I dressed my maids as Amazons and rode bare-breasted halfway to Damascus. Louis had a seizure and I damn near died of windburn...but the troops were dazzled!"

Rosa Parks

(4 February 1913 - 24 October 2005)

Rosa Parks was an African American civil rights activist who challenged the racial segregation that existed in parts of the US by refusing to give up her seat on a bus so that a white person could sit down. Her protest was supported by many other African Americans and sparked the civil rights movement which, in the 1960s, eventually won equal rights.

"Memories of our lives, of our works and our deeds will continue in others."

"Racism is still with us. But it is up to us to prepare our children for what they have to meet, and, hopefully, we shall overcome."

"I would like to be known as a person who is concerned about freedom and equality and justice and prosperity for all people."

Susan Sontag

(16 January 1933 - 28 December 2004)

Susan Sontag was a writer and filmmaker. Famous for a string of influential essays including 1964's Notes on 'Camp', Sontag's work embraced such diverse interests as sexuality, art and philosophy. Her decades-spanning career also saw her work as a teacher, political activist and filmmaker.

"Mallarme said that everything in the world exists in order to end in a book. Today everything exists to end in a photograph."

"The only interesting answers are those which destroy the questions."

"What is most beautiful in virile men is something feminine; what is most beautiful in feminine women is something masculine."

Hypatia

(c355 - 415)

Hypatia was an ancient Greek Philosopher. An Alexandrian mathematician, astronomer and philosopher whose murder in AD 415 led to her being enshrined during the Enlightenment as a martyr for philosophy. She is the first female mathematician of whose life and work we have reasonably detailed knowledge.

"Reserve your right to think, for even to think wrongly is better than not to think at all."

"All formal dogmatic religions are fallacious and must never be accepted by self-respecting persons as final."

"Life is an unfoldment, and the further we travel the more truth we can comprehend. To understand the things that are at our door is the best preparation for understanding those that lie beyond."

Artemisia Gentileschi

(8 July 1593 - 1652/53)

Artemisia Gentileschi was an Italian Baroque painter. An accomplished painter in a period of Italy's history when women weren't always welcomed by patrons or fellow artists, Gentileschi generated both critical praise and international success. Her portraits of strong, suffering women represent, for some, the trials she faced in her personal and professional life.

"I have made a solemn vow never to send my drawings because people have cheated me. In particular, just today I found… that, having done a drawing of souls in Purgatory for the Bishop of St. Gata, he, in order to spend less, commissioned another painter to do the painting using my work. If I were a man, I can't imagine it would have turned out this way."

"As long as I live I will have control over my being."

"My illustrious lordship, I'll show you what a woman can do."

Cleopatra

(69 BC - 30 BC)

Cleopatra was an Egyptian Pharaoh. Final ruler of Egypt's Ptolemaic dynasty, Cleopatra was more than the famous beauty her subsequent, simplistic portrayals often depict. A formidable, politically shrewd monarch, she was directly involved in the running of a kingdom that faced challenges on many fronts.

"Celerity is never more admired than by the negligent."

"All strange and terrible events are welcome, but comforts we despise."

"Fool! Don't you see now that I could have poisoned you a hundred times had I been able to live without you."

Emmeline Pankhurst

(14 June 1858 - 14 July 1928)

Emmeline Pankhurst founded the Women's Social and Political Union to campaign for the parliamentary vote for women in Edwardian Britain. She roused thousands of women to demand for their democratic right in a mass movement that has been unparalleled in British history.

"Justice and judgment lie often a world apart."

"Trust in God - she will provide."

"Men make the moral code and they expect women to accept it. They have decided that it is entirely right and proper for men to fight for their liberties and their rights, but that it is not right and proper for women to fight for theirs."

Maria Merian

(2 April 1647 - 6 January 1717)

Maria Merian was a naturalist and entomologist. A German-born naturalist and scientific illustrator, Merian defied expectations of the time by leaving an unhappy marriage and running her own business selling her beautiful artwork depicting the life cycles of plants and insects. At a time when women had few opportunities to study science or to travel, Merian made the journey to Suriname in South America to record the exotic wildlife there. Her stunning full colour prints of tropical plants and animals, including bird-eating spiders, vibrantly coloured butterflies and a snake-wrestling caiman, were studied by generations of scientists after her.

"In my youth, I spent my time investigating insects."

"Art and nature shall always be wrestling until they eventually conquer one another so that the victory is the same stroke and line: that which is conquered, conquers at the same time."

Josephine Butler

(13 April 1828 - 30 December 1906)

Josephine Butler brought into open discussion in Victorian Britain the double sexual standard that existed in a male-dominated society. She campaigned successfully for the repeal of the Contagious Diseases Acts which provided for the compulsory and regular medical examination of women believed to be prostitutes, but not their male clients. In later life, she campaigned against child prostitution and international sex trafficking.

"We read of strong men bowed down with woe, weeping as women weep, turning homewards in the heart-sickness of unavailing search, or with a certainty worse than suspense."

"Attempted modifications of an essential evil always fail."

"It is a fact, that numbers even of moral and religious people have permitted themselves to accept and condone in man what is fiercely condemned in woman."

Indira Gandhi

(19 November 1917 - 31 October 1984)

Indira Gandhi was an Indian Prime Minister, the only female prime minister to date. She is remembered for her political steel and often controversial legacy. She ruled the country on two occasions, from 1966 to 1977 and from 1980 until 1984, when she was assassinated by her own bodyguards.

"I do not like carving the world into segments; we are one world."

"The power to question is the basis of all human progress."

"There are two kinds of people, those who do the work and those who take the credit. Try to be in the first group; there is less competition there."

Estée Lauder

(1 July 1908 - 24 April 2004)

Estée Lauder was a global cosmetics company founder. She started her eponymous business with her husband in 1946. Known for her marketing acumen, she built a beauty empire – including brands such as Bobbi Brown and Clinique – which eventually made her one of the richest self-made women in the world.

"I didn't get there by wishing for it or hoping for it, but by working for it."

"If you don't sell, it's not the product that's wrong, it's you."

"Act tough: what others call tough, I call persistent."

Wangari Maathai

(1 April 1940 - 25 September 2011)

Wangari Maathai was a Kenyan environmental activist who founded the Green Belt Movement which campaigned for the planting of trees, environmental conversation, and women's rights. The first woman in East and Central Africa to earn a doctorate degree, Maathai was elected to parliament and appointed assistant minister for Environment and Natural Resources from 2003 - 2005. Her work was internationally recognised when, in 2004, she became the first African woman to receive the Nobel Peace Prize for her contribution to sustainable development, peace, and democracy.

"It is important to nurture any new ideas and initiatives which can make a difference for Africa."

"I am working to make sure we don't only protect the environment, we also improve governance."

"Until you dig a hole, you plant a tree, you water it and make it survive, you haven't done a thing. You are just talking."

Mary Seacole

(23 November 1805 - 14 May 1881)

Mary Seacole was a British-Jamaican business woman and nurse. In her late forties, Mary travelled from her home in Jamaica to Britain to offer her services as a nurse during the Crimean War (1853-56). Despite being turned down, Seacole refused to give up. Funding her own passage to the Crimea, Mary established the British Hotel near Balaclava. Nineteenth-century soldiers had no welfare support and Seacole's hotel provided a comfortable retreat away from battle with accommodation for convalescents and the sick.

"Beside the nettle, ever grows the cure for its sting."

"Death is always terrible—no one need be ashamed to fear it."

"I am not ashamed to confess that I love to be of service to those who need a woman's help. And wherever the need arises—on whatever distant shore—I ask no greater or higher privilege than to minister to it."

Anna Akhmatova

(11 June 1889 - 5 March 1966)

Anna Akhmatova was a Russian Poet. Akhmatova's career as a poet, which spanned a period of war, totalitarianism and revolution, saw her mix the personal with the political to chronicle a tumultuous chapter in Russian history. Her work and sympathies were often met with official opprobrium, and many of those around her were executed, detained or deported.

"Italy is a dream that keeps returning for the rest of your life."

"It is unbearably painful for the soul to love silently."

"You will hear thunder and remember me, and think: she wanted storms."

Mary Wollstonecraft

(27 April 1759 - 10 September 1797)

Mary Wollstonecraft was an English writer and philosopher, championed education and liberation for women. Her book, A Vindication of the Rights of Woman, was published in 1792 and is seen as one of the foundational texts of modern feminism. Written against the backdrop of the French Revolution, it argued for the equality of women to men.

"Virtue can only flourish among equals."

"Make women rational creatures, and free citizens, and they will quickly become good wives; - that is, if men do not neglect the duties of husbands and fathers."

"It is justice, not charity, that is wanting in the world."

Mary Anning

(21 May 1799 - 9 March 1847)

Mary Anning was a paleontologist. Fossils were crucial for convincing Victorian scientists that evolution had taken place over countless millennia – and dinosaurs provided particularly compelling evidence of the earth's long past. The seashore collector Mary Anning was scarcely educated, yet she became one of Britain's leading experts on prehistoric life, scouring the cliffs of Lyme Regis to dig out large skeletons that she sold to eminent London specialists. Her unique palaeontological specimens helped transform beliefs about the origins of life.

"It is large and heavy but... it is the first and only one discovered in Europe."

"The world has used me so unkindly, I fear it has made me suspicious of everyone."

Marie Curie

(7 November 1867 - 4 July 1934)

Marie Curie was a Polish-born French physicist and chemist. She was the first woman to become a teacher at the University of Paris and the first woman to receive 2 Nobel Prizes (Chemistry and Physics). She was a pioneering researcher on radioactivity and the discoverer of two elements, Polonium and Radium.

"Nothing in life is to be feared, it is only to be understood. Now is the time to understand more, so that we may fear less."

"Be less curious about people and more curious about ideas."

"One never notices what has been done; one can only see what remains to be done."

Joan of Arc

(1412 - 30 May 1431)

Joan of Arc was a Martyr and Military Leader. Joan was born in 1412, nearly 80 years into the Hundred Years' War, which had seen the English take control of a large portion of France. She convinced the future French King Charles VII that religious visions had instructed her to support him. Aged just 17, she was sent to the Siege of Orléans. When the siege was lifted shortly afterwards, Joan became a religious figurehead for a renewed French offensive, helping to achieve further French victories and advising on military strategy. Joan was eventually captured by the Burgundians and put into English custody. In 1431, she was found guilty of heresy and burned at the stake. She became a French martyr and was canonised in 1909.

"I am not afraid... I was born to do this."

"Get up tomorrow early in the morning, and earlier than you did today, and do the best that you can. Always stay near me, for tomorrow I will have much to do and more than I ever had, and tomorrow blood will leave my body above the breast."

Sirimavo Bandaranaike

(17 April 1916 - 10 October 2000)

Sirimavo Bandaranaike was the Prime Minister of Sri Lanka. As socialist, she became the first female head of government in the world when she became Prime Minister of Sri Lanka, in 1960. She served three terms in this capacity: 1960–65, 1970–77 and 1994–2000. Bandaranaike was an important role model for many political female activists, showing that the glass ceiling which prevented women from reaching the highest political office, could be broken.

"It was far from my mind to achieve any personal glory for myself when I assumed the leadership of the party at the request of its leaders."

"As a woman and mother, I call upon the nations of the world to desist from violence in their dealings with each other."

"History is full of examples of the disastrous consequences that came upon such nations that changed their constitutions by giving one man too much power."

Clara Schumann

(13 September 1819 - 20 May 1896)

Clara Schumann was a Musician and Composer. One of the foremost pianists of the Romantic period, Schumann's career began as a child prodigy and spanned more than six decades. Her works include concertos, quartets and songs, and she also taught generations of piano students in Frankfurt.

"Why hurry over beautiful things? Why not linger and enjoy them?"

"There is nothing greater than the joy of composing something oneself and then listening to it."

"I wish to lead a life free from care, and I see that I shall be unhappy if I cannot always work at my art."

Sonja Henie

(8 April 1912 - 12 October 1969)

Sonja Henie was a figure skater and a film star. A Norwegian figure skater who dominated her sport and then moved into a successful acting career in Hollywood. At age 10, she won the Norwegian national figure-skating championship and went on to win Olympic gold medals in her sport in 1928, 1932, and 1936, along with 10 World and six European championships. The first woman figure skater to wear skirts above the knee, Henie could spin nearly 80 revolutions. After retiring in 1936, she moved to the US and combined her professional ice show with starring roles in a number of films.

"Jewelry takes people's minds off your wrinkles."

"The world never puts a price on you higher than the one you put on yourself."

"It's a feeling of ice miles running under your blades, the wind splitting open to let you through, the earth whirling around you at the touch of your toe, and speed lifting you off the ice far from all things that can hold you down."

Gwen John

(22 June 1876 - 18 September 1939)

Gwen John was an artist. Born in the Welsh county of Pembrokeshire, John's quiet, understated demeanour, and style of painting were often overshadowed by that of her brother, Augustus. Subsequent reappraisals of her life and career have instead revealed a talented artist whose work is increasingly influential.

"Aloneness is nearer God, nearer reality."

"To be reserved, secretive, with a passionate violence that causes suffering."

"In talking, shyness and timidity distort the very meaning of my words. I don't pretend to know anybody well. People are like shadows to me and I am like a shadow."

Elizabeth Fry

(21 May 1780 - 12 October 1845)

Elizabeth Fry was a Social Reformer. The so-called 'Angel of Prisons', Fry was an English Quaker who led the campaign in the Victorian period to make conditions for prisoners more humane. She also helped to improve the British hospital system and treatment of the insane.

"Punishment is not for revenge, but to lessen crime and reform the criminal."

"When thee builds a prison, thee had better build with the thought ever in thy mind that thee and thy children may occupy the cells."

"I hope, if you should live to grow up, you will endeavour to be very useful and not spend all your time in pleasing yourself."

Joan Robinson

(31 October 1903 - 5 August 1983)

Joan Robinson was one of the most influential female economists of the 20th century. Joan changed our understanding of labour markets showing that by recognising imperfections in markets, we can address hidden unemployment and low wages. In 1979, she became the first woman to be made an honorary fellow of King's College.

"Ideology is like breath: you never smell your own."

"Unequal distribution of income is an excessively uneconomic method of getting the necessary saving done."

"The purpose of studying economics is not to acquire a set of ready-made answers to economic questions, but to learn how to avoid being deceived by economists."

Emily Hobhouse

(9 April 1860 - 8 June 1926)

Emily Hobhouse was a British welfare campaigner during the Second Anglo-Boer War (1899-1902) in South Africa. She raised funds for the many Boer women and children who were displaced by the war and housed by the British in overcrowded camps. After visiting the camps, she submitted a report to British government highlighting the terrible conditions, which resulted in an official inquiry. Emily was one of the first women in history to successfully challenge the British government and raise social awareness for the plight of civilian populations caught up in conflict.

"Histories should be re-written showing how mistaken statesmen have invariably been in leading their countrymen into war, and how little is gained and at what enormous cost."

"It is astonishing that though so long a list of the world's greatest thinkers in all periods have pronounced against war, yet (to this time) no statesmen has appeared capable of abolishing it as a means of settling disputes..."

Lise Meitner

(7 November 1878 - 27 October 1968)

Lise Meitner was an Austrian-born physicist. As a Jewish woman, she was doubly disadvantaged during her scientific career in Nazi Germany. After fleeing to Sweden in 1938, she received a plea for help from her research collaborator when the experiments they had planned together produced some unexpected results. A couple of days later, she had solved the problem – they had unwittingly initiated the break-up of a uranium atom. By 1945, her theoretical conclusions had been realised practically in the atomic bomb.

"You must not blame us scientists for the use which war technicians have put our discoveries."

"Life need not be easy, provided only that it is not empty."

"Science makes people reach selflessly for truth and objectivity; it teaches people to accept reality, with wonder and admiration, not to mention the deep awe and joy that the natural order of things brings to the true scientist."

Marie Stopes

(15 October 1880 - 2 October 1958)

Marie Stopes was an advocate of birth control and sex educator. She was born in Edinburgh, but she studied for a science degree at University College, London. In 1918, she published the highly popular Married Love, a second book titled Wise Parenthood – which dealt explicitly with contraception – appearing shortly after.

"If the world is not safe for babies you are never going to get a democracy worth having."

"Every heart desires a mate."

"You can take no credit for beauty at sixteen. But if you are beautiful at sixty, it will be your soul's own doing."

Simone de Beauvoir

(9 January 1908 - 14 April 1986)

Simone de Beauvoir was a French Writer and Philosopher. De Beauvoir's publication, in 1949, of The Second Sex had a decisive influence on the evolution of post-war feminism. Her declaration that "one is not born but becomes a woman" continues to reverberate in contemporary discussions of gender.

"I wish that every human life might be pure transparent freedom."

"Change your life today. Don't gamble on the future, act now, without delay."

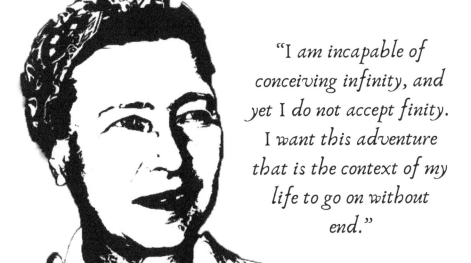

"I am incapable of conceiving infinity, and yet I do not accept finity. I want this adventure that is the context of my life to go on without end."

Maryam Mirzakhani

(3 May 1977 - 14 July 2017)

Maryam Mirzakhani was an Iranian mathematician. She was only 40 when she died, but she had already transcended gender and ethnicity norms by becoming the first woman, and the first Iranian, to win the coveted Fields medal, the mathematics equivalent of the Nobel Prize. Mirzakhani changed the world in her geometrical imagination, calculating the characteristics of countless billiard-table universes, each constantly morphing into different shapes.

"The beauty of mathematics only shows itself to more patient followers."

"I find discussing mathematics with colleagues of different backgrounds one of the most productive ways of making progress."

"I find it fascinating that you can look at the same problem from different perspectives and approach it using different methods."

Emilie du Chatelet

(17 December 1706 - 10 September 1749)

Emilie du Chatelet was a French natural and philosopher. Also a superb mathematician, Emilie du Châtelet did much to convince sceptical Europeans that Isaac Newton's theory of gravity was right. But this mother of three also loved to dance, wear fashionable clothes, and host dinner parties. Her main aim in life, she maintained, was to enjoy herself – and pleasure included the hard grind of intellectual work.

"Love of learning is the most necessary passion ... in it lies our happiness. It's a sure remedy for what ails us, an unending source of pleasure."

"To be happy, one must rid oneself of prejudice, be virtuous, healthy, and have a capacity for enjoyment and for passion."

"Self-love is always the mainspring, more or less concealed, of our actions; it is the wind which swells the sails, without which the ship could not go."

Nellie Bly

(5 May 1864 - 27 January 1922)

Nellie Bly was a pioneering journalist. At a time when women journalists tended to write about domestic topics such as gardening or fashion, Bly wrote hard-hitting stories about the poor and oppressed. In 1886-87, she travelled for several months in Mexico, reporting on official corruption and the condition of the poor, while another investigation saw her feign insanity in order to expose conditions inside asylums. Bly's journalistic fame led her to travel the globe, unchaperoned, in her own Jules Verne inspired 80 Days Around the World. She completed the challenge in 72 days, 6 hours, 11 minutes and 14 seconds, setting a new world record.

"That was the greatest night of my existence. For a few hours I stood face to face with "self!" I"

"Energy rightly applied and directed will accomplish anything."

"It is only after one is in trouble that one realizes how little sympathy and kindness there are in the world."

Frida Kahlo

(6 July 1907 - 3 July 1954)

Frida Kahlo was a Mexican Artist whose striking and distinctive works combine an exploration of gender, class, and identity with symbols from the nation's cultural history. Kahlo has gone on to become an important figure for social causes including feminism and LGBTQ rights.

"I hope the leaving is joyful; and I hope never to return."

"I tried to drown my sorrows, but the bastards learned how to swim, and now I am overwhelmed by this decent and good feeling."

"I never paint dreams or nightmares. I paint my own reality."

Wilma Rudolph

(23 June 1940 - 12 November 1994)

Wilma Rudolph was an olympic champion, an American athlete who was the first black woman to make a major impact on international track and field. She recovered from childhood polio, pneumonia and scarlet fever to win three gold medals at the 1960 Olympic Games, the first American woman to ever do so. Her post-Olympic career included goodwill ambassadorial work for the American government in Africa, as well as campaigning work for the Civil Rights movement.

"I loved the feeling of freedom in running, the fresh air, the feeling that the only person I'm competing with is me."

"I believe in me more than anything in this world."

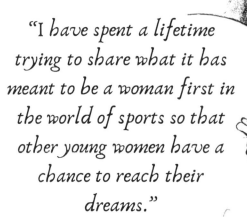

"I have spent a lifetime trying to share what it has meant to be a woman first in the world of sports so that other young women have a chance to reach their dreams."

Aphra Behn

(1640 - 16 April 1689)

Aphra Behn was a British playwright and poet. Apparently prompted to turn to writing after incurring debt from being imprisoned for espionage, Behn was one of the first women in England to earn a living from the profession. Her work was to prove hugely influential, both on literature and for future generations of female writers.

"Love ceases to be a pleasure when it ceases to be a secret."

"Variety is the soul of pleasure."

"Each moment of the happy lover's hour is worth an age of dull and common life."

Catherine of Siena

(25 March 1347 - 29 April 1380)

Catherine of Siena was a Philosopher and Theologian. A mystic and ascetic who in the aftermath of the Black Death played a key role in the campaign to reform the Catholic Church, and return the papacy from Avignon to Rome. She was canonised by Pope Pius II in 1461.

"You are rewarded not according to your work or your time but according to the measure of your love."

"Be who God meant you to be and you will set the world on fire."

"Proclaim the truth and do not be silent through fear."

Suzanne Lenglen

(24 May 1899 - 4 July 1938)

Suzanne Lenglen was a French tennis player who won 21 Grand Slam titles and two Olympic gold medals between 1919 and 1926. In 1920, she became the first person to win three Wimbledon championships – in singles and doubles events – in a single year. Lenglen popularised the sport with her style and flamboyance and became a fashion icon for her style of dress. She was also outspoken against tennis's amateur restrictions and how these kept working-class people out of the sport.

"A little wine tones up the system just right. One cannot always be serious. There must be some sparkle too."

"Should I smile at the prospect of actual poverty and continue to earn a fortune - for whom?"

"There was one day I'll never forget... I'd just turned 12, and my father came back from Compiègne and said: 'Here, I've bought you a tennis racket and some balls. Let's see what you can do in front of a net.'"

Queen Victoria

(24 May 1819 - 22 January 1901)

Victoria remains one of the UK's most iconic monarchs, more than a century after her death, portrayed in countless films and TV series. Crowned in 1837, she oversaw the nation and its empire throughout a remarkable period of social, technological and economic change.

"We are not interested in the possibilities of defeat; they do not exist."

"The important thing is not what they think of me, but what I think of them."

"A marriage is no amusement but a solemn act, and generally a sad one."

Fanny Burney

(13 June 1752 - 6 January 1840)

Fanny Burney was an English novelist and playwright whose self-described "scribblings" were lauded for her skill with satire and caricature. Warm, witty and observant, her work offers valuable insights into high society in 18th-century England.

"Generosity without delicacy, like wit without judgement, generally gives as much pain as pleasure."

"I am ashamed of confessing that I have nothing to confess."

"You must learn not only to judge but to act for yourself."

Isabella Bird

(15 October 1831 - 7 October 1904)

Isabella Bird was an Explorer and Writer. An intrepid 19th-century explorer who defied Victorian conventions of where a lady should go and what a lady should do. After catching the travel bug while on a sea voyage, taken on the orders of doctors to improve her ill health, Bird went on to explore America, Hawaii, Tibet, Malaysia, Japan, India, China, Iran and many more countries. Her journeys were often fraught with danger; she rode thousands of miles on horseback and climbed mountains and volcanoes. The books Bird wrote, and the photographs she took, on the places she visited helped earn her a place as one of the first women to be made a fellow of the Royal Geographical Society.

"I still vote civilization a nuisance, society a humbug and all conventionality a crime."

"A traveller must buy his own experience, and success or failure depends mainly on personal idiosyncrasies."

"I have found a dream of beauty at which one might look all one's life and sigh."

Junko Tabei

(22 September 1939 - 20 October 2016)

Junko Tabei was a Japanese Mountaineer. In 1975, Tabei became the first woman to reach the summit of Mount Everest, a place she described as being "smaller than a tatami mat". It wasn't an easy climb in many respects – Junko faced criticism for leaving her young daughter at home as she set off for Nepal, as part of the first all-female climbing team to be awarded a permit to climb the world's highest peak. News of her astounding feat of human endurance made headlines around the world and Tabei came to stand as a symbol for women's empowerment and challenging female stereotypes.

"Technique and ability alone do not get you to the top - it is the willpower that is the most important. This willpower you cannot buy with money or be given by others - it rises from your heart."

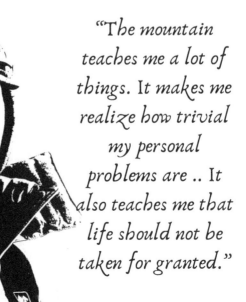

"The mountain teaches me a lot of things. It makes me realize how trivial my personal problems are .. It also teaches me that life should not be taken for granted."

Theodora

(c497 - 28 June 548)

Theodora was an Empress of Byzantium. Theodora exercised considerable influence as wife of the emperor Justinian I, handling political affairs and corresponding with foreign rulers. She is remembered as one of the first rulers to recognise the rights of women, altering divorce laws to give greater benefits to women and prohibiting the traffic in young girls.

"I suddenly realized I was a writer of wide reputation and most of it bad."

"For a king, death is better than dethronement and exile."

"For my own part, I adhere to the maxim of antiquity, that the throne is a glorious sepulchre."

Fanny Blankers-Koen

(26 April 1918 - 25 January 2004)

Fanny Blankers-Koen was a Dutch track and field athlete who won four gold medals at the 1948 Olympic Games in London, along with five European Championship golds between 1946 and 1950. While the press dubbed her 'the flying housewife', the fact that she had two children before her 1948 triumphs helped to undermine the popular notion that being a mother and being an elite athlete were mutually exclusive.

"I remember thinking how strange that I had made so many people happy."

"All I've done is run fast. I don't see why people should make much fuss about that."

"But times were harsh and people were glad of the opportunity to celebrate anything. It made me proud to know I had been able to bring joy into people's lives."

Margaret Thatcher

(13 October 1925 - 8 April 2013)

Margaret Thatcher was Britain's first female prime minister who came to power at an unsettled time in the country's history, as it faced political disharmony and economic recession. Further trials, including the 1982 Falklands War and the conflict in Northern Ireland, helped to define her influential career.

"I love argument, I love debate. I don't expect anyone just to sit there and agree with me, that's not their job."

"If you want something said, ask a man; if you want something done, ask a woman."

"I do not know anyone who has got to the top without hard work. That is the recipe. It will not always get you to the top, but should get you pretty near."

Zora Neale Hurston

(7 January 1891 - 28 January 1960)

Zora Neale Hurston was an African-American author. Hurston's work chronicles life in the American South, particularly the racial and gender struggles she witnessed and experienced during the first half of the 20th century. Her career as an anthropologist also saw her make key contributions to the study of North American folklore and ritual activity in the Caribbean.

"Those that don't got it, can't show it. Those that got it, can't hide it."

"No matter how far a person can go the horizon is still way beyond you."

"It seems that fighting is a game where everybody is the loser."

Gabriela Mistral

(7 April 1889 - 10 January 1957)

Lucila Godoy Alcayaga, known pseudonymously as Gabriela Mistral, was a Chilean poet and diplomat whose works often explore morality and motherhood. She was awarded the Nobel Prize for literature in 1945, becoming the first Latin American author to receive the honour.

"Love that stammers, that stutters, is apt to be the love that loves best."

"You shall create beauty not to excite the senses but to give sustenance to the soul."

"Speech is our second possession, after the soul-and perhaps we have no other possession in this world."

Catherine the Great

(2 May 1729 - 17 November 1796)

Catherine the Great was an Empress of Russia. Russia's longest-ruling female leader, Catherine was head of the country as it modernised, expanded, and strengthened. A patron of arts and a supporter of education, her reforms led her to become one of the most influential rulers in Russian history.

"Power without a nation's confidence is nothing."

"The more a man knows, the more he forgives."

"A great wind is blowing, and that gives you either imagination or a headache."

Sacagawea

(May 1788 - 20 December 1812)

Sacagawea was a Shoshone interpreter. As a female Native American, Sacagawea's story could easily have been lost to history. But her role as a vital member of Lewis and Clark's Corps of Discovery, helping them forge relationships with Native Americans all while carrying her newborn baby on her back, ensured this wasn't the case. Sacagawea travelled thousands of miles with the Lewis and Clark expedition of 1804-6 – from the Mandan-Hidatsa villages in the Dakotas to the Pacific Northwest – acting as an interpreter and allaying the suspicions of the tribes they encountered.

"Everything I do is for my people."

"Amazing the things you find when you bother to search for them."

"Don't go around saying the world owes you a living."

Katharine Graham

(16 June 1917 - 17 July 2001)

Katharine Graham was the Publisher of the Washington Post from 1969–79. She was the first female publisher of a major American newspaper after she took the helm of the Washington Post Company in 1963, after the death of her husband. Graham was also the first female CEO of a Fortune 500 company after taking the company public in 1972. In 1971, she oversaw the publication of the Pentagon Papers and coverage of the Watergate scandal that toppled President Nixon.

"A mistake is simply another way of doing things."

"If one is rich and one's a woman, one can be quite misunderstood."

"The thing women must do to rise to power is to redefine their femininity. Once, power was considered a masculine attribute. In fact, power has no sex."

Ethel Smyth

(22 April 1858 - 8 May 1944)

Ethel Smyth was a composer and suffragist. An English author, composer and campaigner for women's rights, Smyth composed the song that was to become the anthem of the suffrage movement. She was awarded a damehood in 1922 for her work in the fields of music and literature.

"The charms of seclusion are seldom combined with the conveniences of civilization."

"If you take passionate interest in a subject, it is hard not to believe yourself specially equipped for it."

"I feel I must fight for [my music], because I want women to turn their minds to big and difficult jobs; not just to go on hugging the shore, afraid to put out to sea."

Marie Marvingt

(20 February 1875 - 14 December 1963)

Marie Marvingt was a French athlete and aviator. A world class sportswoman and qualified pilot, Marie worked as a Red Cross nurse during the First World War. At one point she joined the French infantry posing as a man and later joined an Italian alpine regiment. In 1915, she piloted a bombing raid over Germany and was awarded the Croix de Guerre. Before the war, Marvingt had begun developing plans for an air ambulance and in the 1930s she devised training for in-flight nurses, vital work that led to a female air ambulance service in the Second World War.

"What is everybody's business is nobody's business."

"This new sport is comparable to no other. It is, in my opinion, one of the most intoxicating forms of sport, and will, I am sure, become one of the most popular. Many of us will perish before then, but that prospect will not dismay the braver spirits. ... It is so delicious to fly like a bird!"

Yeshe Tsogyal

(757 - 817)

Yeshe Tsogyal was the Mother of Tibetian Buddhism. A Tibetan princess who in the 8th century had a defining influence on the development of Buddhism. She is commemorated by her followers as a female Buddha, and named the Victorious Ocean of Wisdom.

"I see nothing to fear in inner space."

"This body is the seat of all good and bad."

"Meditate upon the teacher as the glow of your awareness, When you melt and mingle together, Taste that expanse of nonduality. There remain."

Florence Nightingale

(12 May 1820 - 13 August 1910)

Florence Nightingale led the first official team of British military nurses to Turkey during the Crimean War, fought between Britain and Russia (1853-56). More soldiers died from disease than wounds in this conflict and Nightingale – as well as tending the sick – reported back to the army medical services on how to reduce avoidable deaths.

"How very little can be done under the spirit of fear."

"Peace begins with a smile on your face"

"I attribute my success to this - I never gave or took any excuse."

"The greatest heroes are those who do their duty in the daily grind of domestic affairs whilst the world whirls as a maddening dreidel."

Andrea Dworkin

(26 September 1946 - 9 April 2005)

Andrea Dworkin was a radical feminist and writer. One of the most controversial of modern feminist thinkers, the very radicalism of Dworkin's writings on heterosexuality and pornography (the latter she believed to be a weapon used by men to control women) has ensured that her influence on contemporary debates on gender – while massive – has tended to be occluded.

> *"Feminism is hated because women are hated. Anti-feminism is a direct expression of misogyny; it is the political defense of women hating."*

> *"Only when manhood is dead - and it will perish when ravaged femininity no longer sustains it - only then will we know what it is to be free."*

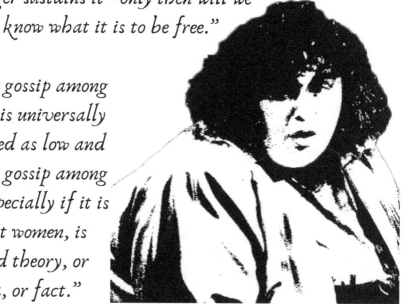

> *"While gossip among women is universally ridiculed as low and trivial, gossip among men, especially if it is about women, is called theory, or idea, or fact."*

Beulah Louise Henry

(11 February 1887 - 1 February 1973)

Beulah Louise Henry was a Prolific Inventor. Known as Lady Edison for her prolific inventions (after the famous inventor Thomas Edison), Henry is credited with more than 100 inventions including the vacuum ice cream freezer and a bobbin-free sewing machine. She founded two of her own companies and served as a consultant to several others.

"If necessity is the mother of invention, then resourcefulness is the father."

"I invent because I cannot help it - new things just thrust themselves on me."

Eleanor Rathbone

(12 May 1872 - 2 January 1946)

Eleanor Rathbone was an MP and Philantrophist. A humanitarian and suffragist, member of the law-abiding National Union of Women's Suffrage Societies (the National Union of Societies for Equal Citizenship from 1919), Rathbone was returned to the British Parliament in 1929 as the Independent Member for the Combined British Universities. She was a key figure in getting through parliament a family allowances bill that paid the allowance to the mother, not the father. During later years, she was actively involved in refugee relief work, trying to rescue Spanish republicans and Jews threatened by Hitler's rise to power.

"... the struggle for the right to become politicians in itself made women into politicians."

"There is, I suppose, no occupation in the world which has an influence on the efficiency and happiness of the members of nearly all other occupations so continuous and so permeating as that of the working housewife and mother."

Murasaki Shikibu

(c978 - 1016)

Murasaki Shikibu was a Japanese novelist and poet. An 11th-century Japanese writer and lady-in-waiting, Shikibu's early talent for Chinese allowed her to become fluent in the language to an extent unusual for women of the period. Her novel The Tale of Genji is widely regarded as a masterpiece.

"There are as many sorts of women as there are women".

"Beauty without colour seems somehow to belong to another world".

"It is useless to talk with those who do not understand one and troublesome to talk with those who criticize from a feeling of superiority. Especially one-sided persons are troublesome. Few are accomplished in many arts and most cling narrowly to their own opinion".

Eleanor Roosevelt

(11 October 1884 - 7 November 1962)

Eleanor Roosevelt was the longest-serving American First Lady (1933-1945), the wife of Franklin D. Roosevelt, 32nd president of the United States, and a United Nations diplomat and humanitarian. She was, in her time, one of the world's most widely admired and powerful women.

"You can often change your circumstances by changing your attitude."

"You must do the things you think you cannot do."

"Tomorrow is a mystery. Today is a gift. That is why it is called the present."

Sojourner Truth

(1797 - 26 November 1883)

Sojourner Truth was a famous African-American abolitionist and women's rights activist best-known for her speech on racial inequalities, "Ain't I a Woman?", delivered extemporaneously in 1851 at the Ohio Women's Rights Convention. Emancipated from slavery by New York state law in 1827, she served as an itinerant preacher before becoming involved in the anti-slavery and women's rights movements.

"Religion without humanity is very poor human stuff."

"Truth is powerful and it prevails."

"It is the mind that makes the body."

Eva Perón

(7 May 1919 - 26 July 1952)

Eva Perón, popularly known as Evita, was the second wife of Argentine president Juan Perón. She became a powerful though unofficial political leader during her husband's first term as president (1946-1952), revered by the lower economic classes.

"Where there is a worker, there lies a nation."

"When the rich think about the poor, they have poor ideas."

"I know that like every woman of the people, I have more strength than I appear to have, I know that like every woman of the people, I have more strength than I appear to have."

Golda Meir

(3 May 1898 - 8 December 1978)

Golda Meir was an Israeli politician born in Ukraine. She and her family immigrated to Milwaukee, Wisconsin, where she became an active Zionist. She helped found the State of Israel in 1948 and later served as its fourth prime minister (1969-1974), becoming the first woman to hold the title.

"One cannot and must not try to erase the past merely because it does not fit the present."

"To be or not to be is not a question of compromise. Either you be or you don't be."

"Those who do not know how to weep with their whole heart don't know how to laugh either"

Corazon Aquino

(25 January 1933 - 1 August 2009)

Corazon Aquino was the first female president of the Philippines, serving from 1986-1992. She was the most prominent figure of the 1986 People Power Revolution, which ended the 21-year rule of President Ferdinand Marcos. She was named Time magazine's Woman of the Year in 1986.

"It is true you cannot eat freedom and you cannot power machinery with democracy. But then neither can political prisoners turn on the light in the cells of a dictatorship."

"One must be frank to be relevant."

"Faith is not simply a patience that passively suffers until the storm is past. Rather, it is a spirit that bears things - with resignations, yes, but above all, with blazing, serene hope."

Millicent Fawcett

(11 June 1847 - 5 August 1929)

Millicent Fawcett was an English leading suffragist and campaigner for equal rights for women. She led Britain's biggest suffrage organisation, the non-violent (NUWSS) and played a key role in gaining women the vote. She also helped found Newnham College, Cambridge, one of the first English university colleges for women.

"What draws men and women together is stronger than the brutality and tyranny which drive them apart."

"Courage calls to courage everywhere, and its voice cannot be denied."

"However benevolent men may be in their intentions, they cannot know what women want and what suits the necessities of women's lives as well as women know these things themselves."

Rosa Luxemburg

(5 March 1871 - 15 January 1919)

Rosa Luxemburg was a Polish/German Marxist theorist, philosopher, economist, anti-war activist, and revolutionary who sought to bring social reform to Germany. She wrote fiercely against German imperialism and for international socialism. In 1919, she was murdered after a failed attempt to bring about a Communist revolution in Germany.

"Those who do not move, do not notice their chains."

"Freedom is always and exclusively freedom for the one who thinks differently."

"The most revolutionary thing one can do is always to proclaim loudly what is happening."

Benazir Bhutto

(21 June 1953 - 27 December 2007)

Benazir Bhutto was a Pakistani politician who became the first female prime minister of a Muslim country. She helped to move Pakistan from a dictatorship to democracy, becoming Prime Minister in 1988 until 1990, and later again from 1993 to 1996. She sought to implement social reforms, in particular helping women and the poor. She was assassinated in 2007.

"Democracy needs support, and the best support for democracy comes from other democracies."

"You can imprison a man, but not an idea. You can exile a man, but not an idea. You can kill a man, but not an idea."

"I believe that democracies do not go to war; that's the lesson of history, and I think that a democratic Pakistan is the world community's best guarantee of stability in Asia."

Marie Antoinette

(2 November 1755 - 16 October 1793)

Maria Antonia Josepha Joanna, better known as Marie Antoinette, was the last Queen of France who helped provoke the popular unrest that led to the French Revolution and to the overthrow of the monarchy in August 1792. She was born in Austria and, at a young age, married to King Louis XVI of France.

"There is nothing new except what has been forgotten."

"I have seen all, I have heard all, I have forgotten all."

"Courage! I have shown it for years; think you I shall lose it at the moment when my sufferings are to end?"

Hildegard of Bingen

(1098 - 17 September 1179)

Hildegard of Bingen was a medieval mystic and visionary and Abbess of Bingen's Benedictine community, a powerful figure within the church. She was also a prolific composer and the author of several books on spirituality, visions, medicine, health and nutrition, nature. She was made a saint of the Church of England and was later canonized by the Catholic Church.

"The mystery of God hugs you in its all-encompassing arms."

"Glance at the sun. See the moon and stars. Gaze at the beauty of the green earth. Now think."

"Humanity, take a good look at yourself. Inside, you've got heaven and earth, and all of creation. You're a world— everything is hidden in you."

Ida Bell Wells-Barnett

(16 July 1862 - 25 March 1931)

Ida Bell Wells-Barnett, better known as Ida B. Wells, was an African American journalist, abolitionist and feminist who led an anti-lynching crusade in the United States in the 1890s. She went on to found and become integral in groups striving for African American justice.

"Virtue knows no color line."

"The way to right wrongs is to turn the light of truth upon them."

"One had better die fighting against injustice than die like a dog or a rat in a trap."

Emily Murphy

(14 March 1868 - 27 October 1933)

Emily Murphy was a Canadian women's rights activist, jurist, and author. In 1916, she became the first female magistrate in Canada, and in the British Empire. In 1927 she joined forces with four other Canadian women who sought to challenge an old Canadian law that said, "women should not be counted as persons" This paved the way for women to enter Parliament and gain greater equality.

"Nothing ever happens by chance; everything is pushed from behind."

"No woman can become or remain degraded without all women suffering."

"We want women leaders today as never before. Leaders who are not afraid to be called names and who are willing to go out and fight. I think women can save civilization. Women are persons."

Harriet Tubman

(March 1822 - 10 March 1913)

Harriet Tubman was an American escaped slave who became a leading figure in the abolitionist movement. She also served as a spy for the US army during the civil war and was an active participant in the struggle for women's suffrage.

"I freed a thousand slaves; I could have freed a thousand more if only they knew they were slaves."

"Every great dream begins with a dreamer. Always remember, you have within you the strength, the patience, and the passion to reach for the stars to change the world."

"I had crossed the line. I was free; but there was no one to welcome me to the land of freedom. I was a stranger in a strange land."

Kate Sheppard

(10 March 1847 - 13 July 1934)

Kate Sheppard was the most prominent female suffrage leader in New Zealand. Born in England, she headed the Women's Christian Temperance Movement and ran "The White Ribbon" – the country's first women's paper. She organised petitions and wrote to prominent leaders in society. Her campaign was very successful and in 1893, New Zealand became the first country to give women a universal franchise.

"Do not think your single vote does not matter much. The rain that refreshes the parched ground is made up of single drops."

"All that separates, whether of race, class, creed, or sex, is inhuman, and must be overcome."

"The question for me is whether we can keep Earth a safe, pleasant place for humankind and the ecosystems we rely on."

Olympe de Gouges

(7 May 1748 - 3 November 1793)

Olympe de Gouges was a French writer and activist who promoted women's rights and the abolition of slavery. Her most famous work was the "Declaration of the Rights of Woman and the Female Citizen," the publication of which resulted in Gouges being tried and convicted of treason. She was executed in 1783 during the Reign of Terror.

"Women, wake up; the tocsin of reason sounds throughout the universe; recognize your rights."

"Regardless of what barriers confront you, it is in your power to free yourselves; you have only to want to."

"Woman is born free and lives equal to man in her rights. Social distinctions can be based only on the common utility."

Christina

(18 December 1626 - 19 April 1689)

Christina, Queen of Sweden, reigned for nearly 22 years, from 1632 to 1654. She's remembered for her abdication and her conversion from Lutheranism to Roman Catholicism. She also was known for being an unusually well-educated woman for her time, with deep interest in religion, philosophy, arts, mathematics, and alchemy.

"We read for instruction, for correction, and for consolation."

"I love the storm and fear the calm."

"It is a far greater happiness to obey no one than to rule the whole world."

Madame de Stael

(22 April 1766 - 14 July 1817)

Germaine de Staël, known as Madame de Staël, was a French-Swiss woman of letters, political propagandist, and conversationalist, who epitomized the European culture of her time, bridging the history of ideas from Neoclassicism to Romanticism. She also gained fame by maintaining a salon for leading intellectuals. Her writings include novels, plays, moral and political essays, literary criticism, history, autobiographical memoirs, and even a number of poems.

"Love is the whole history of a woman's life, it is but an episode in a man's."

"We understand death for the first time when he puts his hand upon one whom we love."

"Love is the emblem of eternity; it confounds all notion of time; effaces all memory of a beginning, all fear of an end."

Sophie Germain

(1 April 1776 - 27 June 1831)

Sophie Germaine was a French mathematician, physicist, and philosopher. As a mathematician, she contributed notably to the study of acoustics, elasticity, and the theory of numbers. The French Academy of Sciences awarded her a prize for a paper on the patterns produced by vibration.

"Algebra is but written geometry and geometry is but figured algebra."

"It matters little who first arrives at an idea, rather what is significant is how far that idea can go."

"Algebra is nothing more than geometry, in words; geometry is nothing more than algebra, in pictures."

Jane Addams

(6 September 1860 - 28 May 1935)

Jane Addams was a famous American activist, social worker, author, and Nobel Peace Prize winner. She was best known for founding the Hull House in Chicago. Hull House was a progressive social settlement aimed at reducing poverty by providing social services and education to working class immigrants and laborers.

"Action indeed is the sole medium of expression for ethics."

"Civilization is a method of living, an attitude of equal respect for all men."

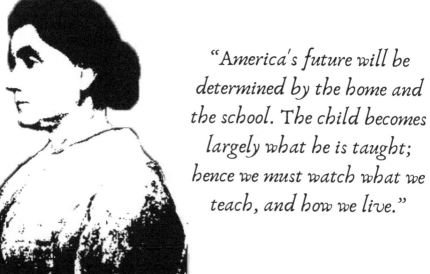

"America's future will be determined by the home and the school. The child becomes largely what he is taught; hence we must watch what we teach, and how we live."

Saint Teresa of Ávila

(28 March 1515 - 4 October 1582)

Teresa of Ávila was a Spanish noblewoman who chose a monastic life in the Catholic Church. As mystic, poet and Carmelite reformer, she lived through the Spanish inquisition but avoided being placed on trial despite her mystical revelations. She helped to reform the tradition of Catholicism and steer the religion away from fanaticism.

"There are more tears shed over answered prayers than over unanswered prayers."

"Be gentle to all and stern with yourself."

"All things must come to the soul from its roots, from where it is planted."

Saint Teresa of Ávila

(28 March 1515 - 4 October 1582)

Teresa of Ávila was a Spanish noblewoman who chose a monastic life in the Catholic Church. As mystic, poet and Carmelite reformer, she lived through the Spanish inquisition but avoided being placed on trial despite her mystical revelations. She helped to reform the tradition of Catholicism and steer the religion away from fanaticism.

"There are more tears shed over answered prayers than over unanswered prayers."

"Be gentle to all and stern with yourself."

"All things must come to the soul from its roots, from where it is planted."

The End

CPSIA information can be obtained
at www.ICGtesting.com
Printed in the USA
BVHW031212221219
567502BV00001B/324/P